AF447943

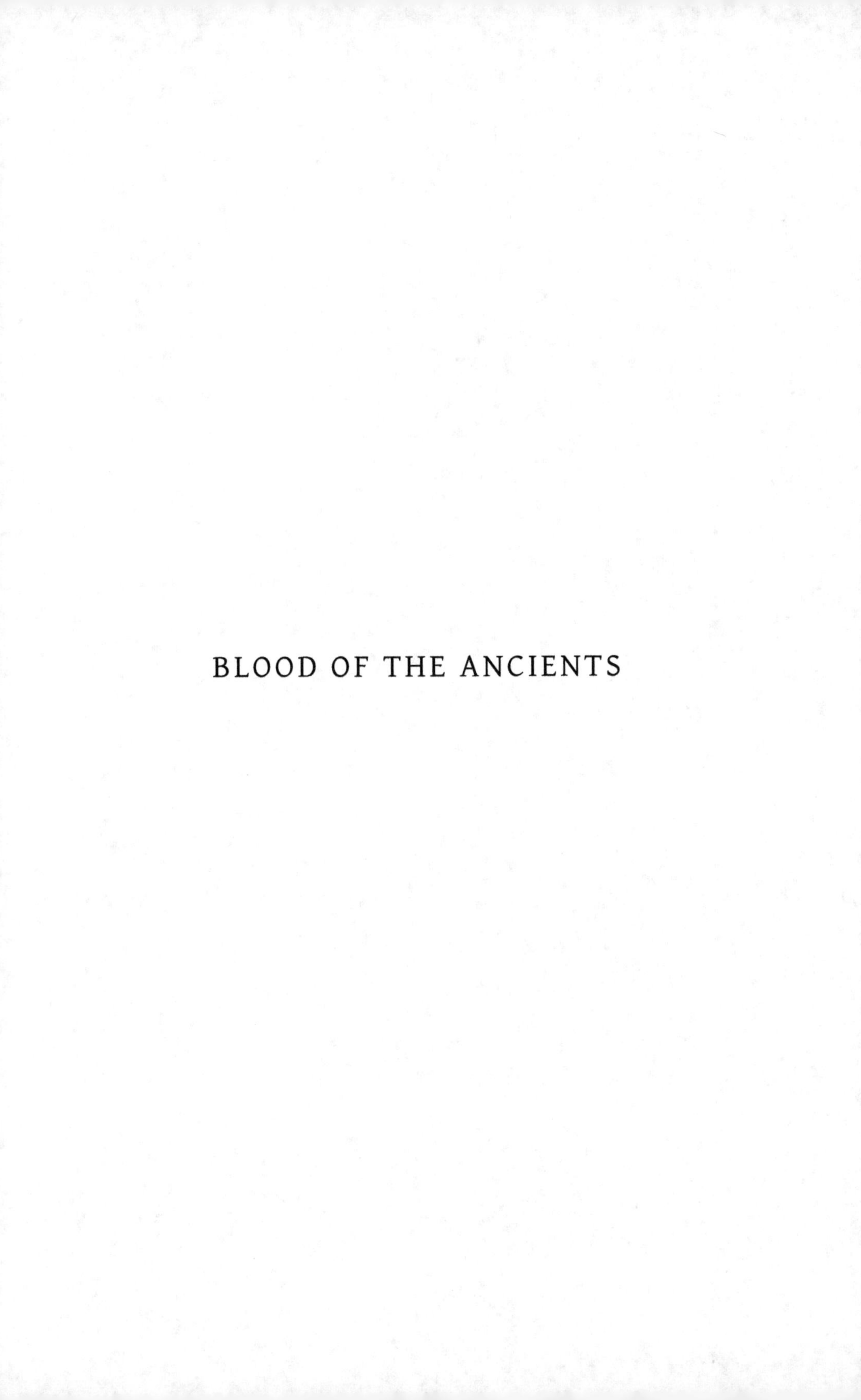

BLOOD OF THE ANCIENTS

Blood of the Ancients

DEMETRI WELSH

CONTENTS

~~

To the ancestors whose voices were silenced,
To the gods and goddesses whose power was buried,
And to the seekers who are unafraid to uncover the truth.

This book is for the rebels, the outcasts, and the wild ones.

For those who know that history is written by the victors,
But the truth is whispered in the dark, beneath the earth,
In rituals of blood, fire, and magic.

For Caleb—though they tried to erase us, our bond is eternal.

Introduction: The Hidden Bloodlines of Celebration

Let me start by asking you a simple question: Do you really know what you're celebrating? I'm not talking about the surface-level answers—the ones you've been spoon-fed since childhood, about the resurrection of Christ or the gathering of pilgrims. I'm asking you to dig deeper. Look beyond the glossy greeting cards, the fairy lights, the chocolate bunnies, and the fireworks. When you raise that glass of champagne on New Year's Eve or tuck into your turkey on Thanksgiving, do you ever stop and wonder: *Where the hell did these traditions come from?*

Because here's the hard truth: the holidays we celebrate today aren't as innocent or as pure as you've been led to believe. Beneath the sanitized Christian veneer lies something far older, far darker, and far more powerful. Each modern holiday—Easter, Christmas, Halloween, even Valentine's Day—is the bastard child of ancient pagan festivals, born of blood, fire, sex, death, and magic. The celebrations of today are echoes of rituals that were raw and untamed, celebrating forces of nature, gods, and goddesses long before anyone heard the name Jesus Christ. The holidays you've grown up with are nothing more than a giant rebranding effort by the Church—a well-executed PR move that, over the centuries, has morphed powerful pagan traditions into something palatable for the masses.

And we bought into it. Hook, line, and sinker. We've been led to believe that Christmas is about the birth of a savior, that Easter is about salvation, and that Thanksgiving is some idyllic tale of harmony between colonists and Native Americans. Bullshit. These stories are about as real as the jolly man in the red suit who supposedly flies down your chimney every December. The truth, buried beneath centuries of religious control and consumer-driven propaganda, is that these celebrations are far older than Christianity, and they're not as "holy" as you might think.

In this book, we're not going to tiptoe around the delicate sensibilities of organized religion, and we sure as hell aren't going to sugarcoat the truth. We're going to tear down the shiny, plastic wrapping of modern holidays and expose their dark, primal cores. We'll go back to the ancient world, to civilizations that celebrated the raw forces of nature, where gods demanded blood and fertility rites ensured the survival of the tribe. We're going to pull these holidays apart piece by piece, unraveling centuries of lies, manipulation, and deceit, to show you that the holidays you think you know are rooted in practices so ancient, so primal, that they still hold sway over us even today.

Think about it. Why are we so obsessed with Easter eggs and rabbits? What's the real story behind Halloween costumes and pumpkins? Why the hell do we cut down trees and bring them into our homes in December, only to throw them out a few weeks later? Every single one of these traditions has a much deeper meaning than you've been told. They're echoes of rites and rituals meant to honor the changing of the seasons, the balance between life and death, the cycles of the earth. They're the remnants of pagan festivals that the Church tried—and ultimately failed—to completely stamp out.

What the early Christian leaders realized is that they couldn't simply destroy the pagan traditions that people had celebrated for millennia. These rituals were too deeply ingrained in the fabric of human culture. So, instead of wiping them out, they did something far more clever—they hijacked them. They rebranded these ancient festivals, slapping Christian narratives on top of them and hoping no one would notice. Christmas? It's a sanitized version of Yule, an ancient winter solstice festival. Easter? That's a pagan fertility celebration, right down to the eggs and rabbits. Halloween? That's Samhain, a Celtic festival that marked the thinning of the veil between the living and the dead. Even Valentine's Day has roots in the Roman festival of Lupercalia, a fertility celebration filled with blood, lust, and sacrifice.

And that's what we're going to explore in this book: the real, raw, and often shocking history behind each major holiday. We'll trace their origins back to ancient pagan rituals, uncovering the blood sacrifices, the orgiastic rites, and the deep connection between human survival and these seasonal celebrations. We'll expose how Christianity tried to co-opt and sanitize these holidays, transforming them into moral, family-friendly events that still carry the unmistakable scent of their pagan past.

But don't get it twisted—this book isn't about bashing Christianity or any other religion. It's about uncovering the truth that's been hidden in plain sight. It's about connecting the dots between the holidays we celebrate today and the ancient, primal forces that they were originally meant to honor. Whether you're a believer or a skeptic, there's one undeniable fact: the holidays we celebrate now are not the invention of any church or any single religion. They are far older, far more universal, and far more rooted in the human experience than any religious institution could ever claim.

So, buckle up. This journey is going to take us through history, myth, and magic. We're going to visit ancient temples, where blood was spilled in honor of the gods. We're going to walk through the sacred groves where druids once led fire-lit processions under the full moon. We'll step into the chaotic streets of ancient Rome, where Saturnalia turned the world upside down, and we'll witness the sexual rituals of Beltane, where life and death were intertwined in the fires of lust.

And yes, we're going to piss some people off along the way. Some will say this book is sacrilegious, that it's an attack on their faith. Let them. Because the truth is more important than their comfort, and the truth is this: the holidays we celebrate today are pagan to their core. Christianity may have tried to cover them with a veneer of respectability, but beneath that thin layer, the ancient rites and rituals are still very much alive. They pulse through the earth, through the air, through our collective unconscious. They shape the way we celebrate, the way we gather, the way we honor life, death, and everything in between.

So, whether you're lighting candles for Christmas or carving pumpkins for Halloween, know this: you are participating in rituals far older than you've been told. You are tapping into something primal, something ancient, something powerful. And now, it's time to face that truth head-on.

This is *Blood of the Ancients*. Welcome to the real story behind the holidays.

~ 1 ~

THE RESURRECTION OF
FERTILITY – EASTER AND THE
GOD

Let's kick things off with one of the most iconic holidays in the Western world: Easter. If you grew up in a religious household, you probably heard that Easter is the celebration of the resurrection of Jesus Christ—a sacred holiday representing triumph over death and the promise of eternal life. You might have gone to church, attended sunrise services, or watched grand religious processions. And of course, you've probably participated in Easter egg hunts, marveled at pastel-colored baskets, and maybe even wondered why a giant rabbit is hopping around delivering chocolate.

But here's the thing—Easter, in its modern form, is one of the most egregious examples of how Christianity hijacked an ancient pagan festival and warped it into a story of salvation. The truth is, long before anyone whispered the name "Jesus," people were celebrating this time of year in ways that were raw, primal, and deeply connected to the rhythms of life and death. And at the center of this celebration wasn't Christ, but the goddess Ishtar—one of the most powerful and revered deities of the ancient world.

Ishtar: The Goddess of Love, War, and Fertility

Before we can even begin to unravel the tangled history of Easter, we need to talk about Ishtar. Who was she? What did she represent? And why was she so significant to the cultures that worshiped her?

Ishtar was one of the most important goddesses in the ancient Mesopotamian pantheon. Known by different names in different regions (Inanna to the Sumerians, Astarte in other Near Eastern cultures), she was the goddess of love, war, fertility, and sex. A goddess of contradictions, she was both the giver of life and the harbinger of death, the nurturer of fertility and the destroyer of worlds. Her power wasn't just tied to gentle love and fertility, though—she was a goddess who could unleash fury and destruction when crossed. In fact, many of her stories depict her leading armies, demanding blood sacrifices, and seeking vengeance on those who defied her.

But it wasn't just her association with war and love that made Ishtar significant. She was a central figure in the myths surrounding the cycles of death and rebirth, making her a natural fit for the spring equinox celebrations. These festivals—held at the time of year when winter's icy grip finally loosened and the earth began to bloom again—were all about the return of life, fertility, and abundance after the long dark months. And that's where things start to connect to Easter.

The Spring Equinox: A Time of Rebirth

Let's break down what's really happening during the time of year we now associate with Easter. The spring equinox is a moment when the day and night are of equal length, marking the balance between light and darkness. It's a time of transition—the tipping point between the death of winter and the rebirth of spring. This is a universal event, celebrated in some form by nearly every ancient culture across the globe, long before Christianity entered the picture.

For the ancients, the return of the sun and the blossoming of new life weren't just natural phenomena—they were sacred, magical events. In Mesopotamia, this rebirth of the natural world was embodied by Ishtar, the goddess of fertility and life, who represented the renewal of the earth itself. The stories of her descent into the underworld and her triumphant return to the land of the living mirror the very cycle of the seasons—winter as death, spring as rebirth. Sound familiar?

This mythological cycle of death and resurrection predates the story of Jesus by centuries, and yet it's impossible to ignore the parallels. The narrative of a divine being descending into the underworld or dying, only to rise again and bring new life to the earth, is deeply ingrained in the human psyche. It's an archetype that appears across cultures, from Ishtar in Mesopotamia to Osiris in Egypt and, yes, eventually in the figure of Christ.

The Egg and the Rabbit: Symbols of Fertility

Now let's get to the fun part—the eggs and the bunny. What's the deal with these seemingly random symbols that have nothing to do with a man rising from the dead? The truth is, these aren't random at all. They're deeply rooted in ancient fertility rites and are symbols that go way back—long before Christianity laid claim to this season of rebirth.

The egg is one of the oldest and most potent symbols of fertility across multiple ancient cultures. It represents the potential for life, the mystery of creation, and the cyclical nature of birth and rebirth. In pagan festivals associated with the spring equinox, eggs were often used in rituals to honor fertility goddesses like Ishtar. The act of decorating and offering eggs was a form of magical practice meant to ensure the land's fertility for the coming year.

And what about the bunny? Rabbits have long been associated with fertility because, well, they breed like crazy. Their rapid reproduction makes them an obvious symbol for abundance, fertility, and life. In ancient pagan festivals, hares and rabbits were sacred animals connected to goddesses of fertility, and their presence during spring rituals was meant to invoke the fertile energies of the earth.

So when you're hiding chocolate eggs or watching the Easter Bunny bounce around your local mall, what you're really participating in is a centuries-old fertility ritual that was co-opted by Christianity. The rabbit and the egg, symbols of sex and fertility, have absolutely nothing to do with the resurrection of Christ and everything to do with honoring the primal forces of life.

Christianity's Hijacking of Easter

This brings us to the core of the issue: how did a pagan fertility festival celebrating Ishtar and the renewal of life become a holiday about the resurrection of Christ? The answer lies in one of the greatest PR moves in religious history—Christianity's strategic co-opting of existing pagan festivals to ease its expansion.

When Christianity was spreading through Europe and the Near East, it encountered deeply ingrained pagan traditions. Rather than try to destroy these popular festivals outright—an approach that would have led to resistance and rebellion—the early Church decided to absorb and rebrand them. Easter, which aligns with the timing of the spring equinox, was the perfect candidate. By overlaying the story of Christ's resurrection on top of these already established pagan celebrations of death and rebirth, the Church was able to both validate its own narrative and gradually phase out the old religions.

The symbolism of Christ's death and resurrection fit perfectly into the existing framework of spring equinox festivals, which were already focused on themes of life emerging from death. By claiming Easter as a celebration of Christ's return from the grave, the Church effectively erased the older, messier pagan origins of the festival.

But here's the thing—they didn't completely erase it. The eggs, the rabbits, the timing of the holiday itself—all of these elements remain as echoes of the ancient fertility rites that predate Christianity. And while the Church may have rebranded the holiday, the deeper, primal energies associated with this time of year are still very much alive. Whether people realize it or not, they're still participating in the rituals of rebirth and renewal that were originally meant to honor goddesses like Ishtar.

Uncovering the Lost Power of the Equinox

So, what does this all mean? Why does it matter that Easter is rooted in ancient fertility rituals, and why should we care about the goddess Ishtar in the context of a holiday that's supposedly about Jesus? Because understanding the true origins of these celebrations reconnects us with the deeper, more powerful forces that have shaped human culture for millennia.

Easter, at its core, is a time to honor the forces of life, death, and rebirth. It's a celebration of the cyclical nature of existence, the eternal dance between the light and the dark, the old and the new. By uncovering the pagan roots of this holiday, we can reclaim the original power of this season—a power that Christianity tried to subdue but could never fully extinguish.

Ishtar's presence still lingers in every egg, in every rabbit, in every flower that blooms after the long winter. Her story of death and resurrection is older than Christianity and remains a potent reminder of the ancient forces that continue to shape our world, even if we've forgotten their names.

So the next time you celebrate Easter, remember that what you're really celebrating isn't just a sanitized version of resurrection, but the raw, primal energy of fertility, renewal, and life itself—an energy that has pulsed through the earth since the time of Ishtar, and long before the rise of any one religion.

~ 2 ~

YULE AND SATURNALIA – THE REAL CHRISTMAS

Let's shift from the renewal of spring to the deep, dark heart of winter. When you think of Christmas, you probably imagine cozy fireplaces, twinkling lights, and a rosy-cheeked man in a red suit. It's the most magical time of the year, right? But hold on—before you sip your spiked eggnog or hang those stockings by the fire, let me break something down for you.

Christmas isn't what you think it is. It never was. Like Easter, this beloved holiday has a much darker, much older history buried beneath layers of Christian propaganda and consumer-driven fairytales. And what we're left with today—a celebration supposedly honoring the birth of Jesus—is nothing more than a massive rebranding of ancient pagan festivals steeped in debauchery, chaos, and the wild forces of nature.

At the heart of it all is the *Winter Solstice*, the darkest night of the year. This celestial event was celebrated by ancient peoples with rituals of death and rebirth, and more often than not, with a heavy dose of blood, sacrifice, and wild revelry. So grab a seat, because we're going deep into the origins of Christmas, back to two of the most important festivals you've never been taught about: *Yule* and *Saturnalia.*

Yule: The Pagan Festival of the Sun's Return

Long before Christmas trees, stockings, and carols, there was Yule—the winter solstice festival celebrated by the ancient Norse, Germanic, and Celtic peoples. Yule marked the longest night of the year, the point when the sun appeared to die, only to be reborn again as the days slowly began to grow longer. For the pagans of northern Europe, the winter solstice was a time of deep magic, when the veil between the worlds was thin and the forces of death and life intertwined in a cosmic dance.

Yule wasn't just about waiting out the darkness—it was about embracing it. In the ancient world, winter was a time of survival. The crops had long been harvested, the animals slaughtered, and people huddled in their homes, hoping they had enough to make it through the cold months. But Yule brought with it a promise: the return of the sun, the rebirth of the light, and the eventual thaw of the frozen earth.

The symbolism here is powerful. The Yule log, a centerpiece of the holiday, was traditionally a massive oak log brought into the home and burned in the hearth for 12 days. But this wasn't just a cozy tradition; it was a sacred rite meant to bring protection and fertility for the coming year. The oak tree was sacred to the god Thor, and burning the Yule log was a way to honor the gods and ensure survival. Ash from the log was often saved and used in rituals throughout the year, its power believed to hold the essence of the sun itself.

The Wild Hunt and Otherworldly Spirits

Yule wasn't just about fires and feasts; it was also about the supernatural. During the solstice, the boundary between the world of the living and the dead was at its thinnest, allowing spirits and gods to roam freely. One of the most fearsome and awe-inspiring aspects of Yule was the Wild Hunt, a spectral procession led by Odin himself, tearing across the skies with a host of spirits, wolves, and otherworldly beings.

This wasn't a time to be caught wandering alone. The Wild Hunt was said to sweep up any unlucky souls found outside after dark, dragging them into the underworld or the afterlife. People left offerings of food and drink to appease Odin and the spirits of the Hunt, hoping for protection during this dangerous time.

And if you're thinking this sounds a lot like Santa Claus riding through the sky in a sleigh, you're right. The figure of Santa Claus as we know him today is a blend of multiple pagan and folk traditions, with a heavy dose of Christian revisionism thrown in for good measure. The Wild Hunt, Odin's long beard, and the tradition of leaving offerings to appease supernatural beings all found their way into the modern Christmas mythos.

Saturnalia: Rome's Raucous Festival

While the northern Europeans were celebrating Yule, the Romans were throwing one of the wildest festivals in ancient history—Saturnalia. This wasn't some quaint little holiday; Saturnalia was a week-long orgy of excess, chaos, and the complete inversion of social norms. Held in honor of Saturn, the god of agriculture, wealth, and time, Saturnalia marked the end of the harvest and the beginning of winter—a time when the land lay barren and the future uncertain.

For the Romans, Saturnalia was all about turning the world upside down. Slaves became masters, the rich and poor exchanged roles, and the rigid social hierarchy of Roman society was temporarily obliterated. Gambling, feasting, and unrestrained revelry were the order of the day. People wore masks and costumes, obscuring their identities and adding to the sense of chaos. Sound familiar? This topsy-turvy world has echoes in our modern traditions of Christmas parties and New Year's Eve masquerades.

Gifts and Debauchery

One of Saturnalia's lasting legacies is the tradition of gift-giving. During the festival, Romans exchanged tokens, often symbolic or humorous, as a way of spreading goodwill (or sometimes just making a point). But gift-giving wasn't about showing generosity in the way we think of it today. It was part of the larger ritual of role reversal, a symbolic gesture that allowed the lower classes a momentary taste of power before they returned to their subservient roles.

And while today's Christmas celebrations might include some drunken merriment, it's nothing compared to the sheer debauchery of Saturnalia. The Roman festival wasn't just about good-natured partying—it was a complete abandonment of social order, with drinking, feasting, gambling, and sometimes even public sex taking place in the streets. The idea was that by indulging in excess, people could release the built-up tensions of the year and prepare for the lean, hard months of winter to come.

Christianity's Takeover: Hijacking the Solstice

So how did these wild, hedonistic pagan festivals turn into the quaint, cozy Christmas we know today? Like with Easter, Christianity didn't start from scratch—it simply took what was already there and slapped a new narrative on top of it. The Roman Catholic

Church, recognizing that it couldn't erase deeply ingrained pagan traditions, decided to co-opt them instead.

December 25th, the date we now celebrate as Christmas, was chosen because it coincided with the Roman festival of *Dies Natalis Solis Invicti*, or the Birthday of the Unconquered Sun. This was a solar festival celebrating the return of the sun after the winter solstice, a perfect metaphor for the birth of Christ, who was increasingly referred to as the "Light of the World."

But let's be real—the Church knew exactly what it was doing. By placing the birth of Jesus on the same day as an important pagan festival, it made the transition from paganism to Christianity a little smoother. People could keep their same traditions and celebrations, but now they were supposedly honoring Christ instead of the sun god or Saturn.

However, the deeper meaning of the solstice—the celebration of the return of the light after the darkest night—was never truly erased. It's still there, buried under the tinsel and lights, whispering to us from the shadows. Whether you're hanging stockings or stringing up lights, the act of decorating your home for Christmas is an echo of the Yule traditions that honored the forces of nature and sought protection from the darkness.

The Christmas Tree: Pagan Roots in the Forest

One of the most iconic symbols of Christmas is the tree. We drag it into our homes, decorate it with lights and ornaments, and place gifts beneath it, but why? The Christmas tree is yet another holdover from ancient pagan practices. The Norse and Germanic peoples believed that evergreens were magical symbols of life and fertility, able to withstand the harshness of winter. They would decorate trees with offerings of food, candles, and trinkets to honor the gods and ensure the return of the sun.

Bringing an evergreen into the home during the darkest part of the year was a way to invite life and light into the home, a reminder that even in the dead of winter, the forces of life still persisted. When you deck out your Christmas tree with glittering baubles and candy canes, you're participating in an ancient ritual that predates Christianity by centuries.

Santa Claus: A Pagan God in Disguise

Now, let's talk about the man of the season himself: Santa Claus. He's jolly, he's generous, and he supposedly flies through the sky delivering gifts to children around the world. But the truth is, Santa is a patchwork figure made up of various ancient deities, folklore characters, and legends.

At his core, Santa is a modern version of Odin, the Norse god of wisdom, war, and death. Odin was said to lead the Wild Hunt during Yule, flying across the sky with his eight-legged horse, Sleipnir. During the Yule season, Norse children would leave offerings of food for Sleipnir in exchange for blessings from Odin. Sound familiar? Santa's sleigh and reindeer are direct descendants of Odin's mythical ride, and the tradition of leaving out cookies and milk is just a modern twist on leaving offerings for the god.

Even Santa's appearance—his long white beard, his fur-lined cloak—bears a striking resemblance to depictions of Odin and other winter gods. The transformation from ancient god to modern folk figure happened gradually, as elements of Norse mythology were blended with Christian saints like St. Nicholas and local European traditions.

The Return of the Light

At its core, Christmas is still a celebration of light in the darkness, of life emerging from the cold grip of winter. Whether you call it Yule, Saturnalia, or Christmas, the heart of the holiday remains the same: it's about the return of the sun, the renewal of life, and the triumph of light over darkness. The early Christians may have tried to make it all about the birth of Christ, but the echoes of the old ways are still there, hidden in plain sight.

So the next time you gather around the Christmas tree, sip your mulled wine, or give gifts to your loved ones, remember—you're not just participating in a religious holiday. You're engaging in an ancient ritual that spans thousands of years, from the wild forests of the north to the decadent streets of ancient Rome. Christmas, at its core, is pagan to the bone. The Church may have tried to co-opt it, but the spirit of Yule and Saturnalia still pulses beneath the surface, reminding us that the forces of life, death, and rebirth are eternal.

~ 3 ~

SAMHAIN – THE DARK ROOTS OF HALLOWEEN

Now we're getting to the real dark stuff. The kind of holiday that chills you to the bone, and not because of the autumn wind. Halloween. Or should I say *Samhain*—the ancient Celtic festival from which Halloween draws every last drop of its blood-soaked roots. If you think Halloween is just about candy, costumes, and haunted houses, let me tell you—those sanitized versions are nothing more than a pale reflection of the ancient rituals that once marked this time of year. We're talking about communing with the dead, animal sacrifices, fire rites, and the deep belief that, on this night, the boundary between the living and the dead was as thin as a razor's edge.

Forget the candy and plastic costumes—Samhain was a celebration of death and the afterlife. It wasn't a commercialized parade of tricks and treats; it was a solemn, powerful, and terrifying time of the year, one that the ancient Celts approached with a mixture of reverence and dread. This was the time when the dead walked among the living, when spirits could cross over and wreak havoc or offer blessings. It was a festival dedicated to acknowledging and respecting the inevitability of death, but also a time to ensure that life would continue through the long, hard winter ahead.

So, buckle up—we're about to dive into the true story behind Halloween, and trust me, it's a lot darker and more ancient than the version you celebrate today.

Samhain: The Festival of the Dead

Long before Halloween became the sugar-fueled frenzy it is today, it was Samhain (pronounced *Sow-en*), one of the most important festivals in the Celtic calendar. Celebrated on October 31st and into November 1st, Samhain marked the end of the harvest season and the beginning of winter, the dark half of the year. It was a time of transition—both for the living and the dead.

The Celts believed that on Samhain, the veil between the physical world and the spirit world thinned to its most fragile state, allowing the dead to return to the land of the living. This wasn't just metaphorical. For the Celts, the dead were very real, and they could walk among the living on this night. Spirits, faeries, and other supernatural entities roamed the earth, and they could either bless or curse you, depending on how you treated them.

Samhain wasn't a celebration in the way we think of modern holidays—it was a deeply spiritual, almost apocalyptic time. It was about survival, both physical and spiritual. The harvest was over, and winter was coming—a time of darkness, cold, and death. But before the earth plunged into winter's deep freeze, Samhain offered a moment to honor the ancestors, to connect with the dead, and to seek their protection during the hard months ahead.

The festival was also a time of fire—huge bonfires were lit to ward off evil spirits and guide the souls of the dead. People would gather around these fires, burning offerings of food, drink, and livestock to ensure that the spirits were appeased and that the community would be protected. This wasn't just about superstition—this was about survival. In a world where winter often meant death, the rituals of Samhain were a way to ensure that the forces of death didn't claim the living prematurely.

This was the original "Halloween"—a time of fire, blood, and spirits. Nothing about this was light-hearted or fun. The Celts were facing the unknown forces of death, and they knew better than to ignore them.

The Thin Veil: Life and Death Intertwined

One of the central beliefs surrounding Samhain was that the boundary between life and death was almost non-existent during this time. The dead could cross over into the world of the living, and in return, the living could communicate with those who had passed. This wasn't a fun, spooky idea—it was a serious, sacred truth to the ancient Celts.

Because of this, the rituals surrounding Samhain were designed to protect the living from harmful spirits while honoring the dead. Food and drink were left out for wandering spirits to ensure they were appeased. Families would often set extra places at the table for their deceased relatives, believing that they would return for one final meal with their loved ones before crossing back to the other side.

But not all spirits were welcome. Some were dangerous, malevolent entities that needed to be kept at bay. This is where the idea of costumes and masks comes into play. The Celts believed that by wearing costumes—often made of animal skins and heads—they could disguise themselves from harmful spirits who might seek to harm them or take them to the underworld. In other words, you weren't dressing up for fun—you were trying to avoid being recognized by the spirits who might want to drag you back to the land of the dead.

Sound familiar? The costumes and masks of modern Halloween are a direct descendant of these ancient rituals. Only now, instead of wearing them to avoid malevolent spirits, we wear them for fun, unaware of the true meaning behind the tradition.

Fire, Sacrifice, and the Spirits

Fire was central to Samhain. Huge bonfires were lit throughout the villages, acting as a beacon to the spirits of the dead and a way to purify the land. These weren't just decorative fires—they were part of elaborate rituals meant to cleanse the community and protect it from the forces of darkness.

At the end of the harvest season, after the crops had been gathered, livestock that couldn't be kept alive through the winter were slaughtered in a ritualistic manner. Some of these animals were sacrificed as offerings to the gods and the spirits of the dead, their blood spilled to ensure the fertility of the land in the coming spring. The bonfires were also used to burn offerings to the gods—often in the form of food and drink, but sometimes in the form of animals, and possibly even humans in the earlier days of the festival.

Samhain was a time of blood, fire, and death, not because the Celts were morbid or obsessed with death, but because they understood the cycles of nature. Death was necessary to ensure rebirth. The land needed to rest, just as the dead needed to be honored, for the wheel of life to continue turning.

These bonfires weren't just about light and warmth—they were symbolic, deeply magical acts. Fire was believed to be purifying, a force that could drive away evil spirits while simultaneously drawing the souls of the dead toward the living. The Celts would extinguish all hearth fires in their homes before the great bonfires were lit. Then, each family would relight their hearths from the sacred flames of the Samhain bonfire, symbolizing the renewal of light and life for the coming year. This wasn't some quaint tradition—it was a magical act of protection and rebirth.

The fires were also a signal of sacrifice. Animals were offered up to the gods to ensure the survival of the tribe, their blood staining the earth as a necessary offering to the powers that governed life and death. There are even legends, though controversial, suggesting that in the early days of Samhain, human sacrifices may have been made as well. These sacrifices were not seen as evil or barbaric by the Celts; they were a necessary exchange with the gods and the spirits, a way to ensure that life would continue and that the cycle of death and rebirth would remain unbroken.

The Christian Hijacking of Samhain

Like most of the pagan festivals, Samhain didn't go unnoticed by the Christian church as it spread across Europe. The Church, recognizing the deep importance of Samhain to the local people, did what it always did—it hijacked the festival and tried to replace it with a more Christian-friendly narrative. Enter *All Hallows' Eve*, the precursor to Halloween, and *All Saints' Day*, both of which were attempts to Christianize this pagan celebration of the dead.

Pope Gregory III, in the 8th century, moved the feast of All Saints to November 1st, aligning it with Samhain in an obvious attempt to overshadow the pagan holiday with a Christian one. All Hallows' Eve, the night before All Saints' Day, became a time to honor saints and martyrs, but as much as the church tried to suppress the old ways, they couldn't fully stamp out the influence of Samhain. The people continued their traditions of lighting bonfires, leaving offerings for the dead, and wearing costumes to ward off spirits.

The blending of Samhain with Christian practices didn't eradicate the pagan elements; instead, it created the strange hybrid holiday that eventually morphed into the Halloween we recognize today. But don't get it twisted—the core of Halloween, with its focus on death, spirits, and the supernatural, is pure paganism. The church may have slapped its saintly gloss on it, but the roots of this festival are still firmly planted in the blood-soaked earth of Samhain.

Jack-o'-Lanterns and Offerings to the Dead

One of the most iconic symbols of modern Halloween is the jack-o'-lantern, those grinning, grotesque pumpkins that light up windows and doorsteps every October. But like everything else in this holiday, the jack-o'-lantern has its roots in Samhain.

The Celts didn't carve pumpkins—those are a New World crop. Instead, they carved turnips, potatoes, and beets, using them as lanterns to ward off evil spirits. These carved vegetables were meant to act as protection, their eerie faces scaring away the wandering souls and malevolent entities that roamed the earth on Samhain night. The flickering light inside represented both the fires of the underworld and the guiding light for the souls of the dead, helping them find their way back to the spirit realm.

The tradition of offering food to spirits also evolved over time. Originally, families would leave out food and drink as offerings to appease the spirits and prevent them from causing harm. Over time, this practice transformed into what we now know as *trick-or-treating*. Children, dressed as spirits or other supernatural creatures, would go from house to house, receiving offerings (in the form of candy) in exchange for protection—essentially reenacting the ancient custom of placating the wandering dead.

Costumes: Disguising Yourself from the Dead

As we mentioned earlier, the tradition of wearing costumes on Halloween has its origins in the ancient practice of disguising oneself to avoid recognition by harmful spirits. The Celts believed that on Samhain, spirits of the dead—and other malevolent entities—were free to roam the earth. To protect themselves, people would don masks and costumes, hoping to blend in with the supernatural beings and avoid their wrath.

These disguises weren't playful or humorous like they often are today. In fact, the more terrifying the costume, the better. The idea was to make yourself unrecognizable or even scarier than the spirits themselves, tricking them into thinking you were one of them. What's interesting here is that this practice, rooted in fear and protection from the dead, has evolved into a lighthearted tradition in modern times—though the original meaning remains hidden beneath layers of modern consumerism.

The Spirit of Samhain Lives On

Though Halloween today is often seen as a fun, spooky celebration filled with candy, costumes, and parties, the echoes of Samhain still reverberate through its traditions. The focus on death, spirits, and the supernatural, the lighting of lanterns, and the wearing of costumes all tie back to the ancient belief that on this night, the veil between the worlds was at its thinnest.

But modern Halloween has lost its deeper connection to death and the afterlife. The original meaning of Samhain wasn't about cheap scares or sugary treats—it was about facing the reality of death, honoring the spirits of the dead, and acknowledging the cyclical nature of life. It was a time of deep spirituality, a time when people recognized their connection to the earth, to their ancestors, and to the forces beyond their understanding.

While we may not gather around bonfires to sacrifice animals or leave out offerings for the dead, the spirit of Samhain is still there, lurking beneath the surface. Whether we realize it or not, when we light jack-o'-lanterns, dress in costumes, or celebrate the eerie, we're participating in rituals that are thousands of years old. The energy of Samhain, with its focus on death, rebirth, and the spirit world, still pulses through Halloween, even if most people have forgotten its origins.

Conclusion: Embracing the Dark Side of Halloween

Halloween isn't just about scares and sweets—it's the remnant of one of the most ancient and profound celebrations of death and the afterlife. Samhain, with its fire rituals, sacrifices, and spiritual connections, was a time when people faced the reality of death head-on and honored the forces that governed life itself. The Christian church may have tried to overlay it with All Saints' Day and All Hallows' Eve, but the essence of Samhain is still alive in the shadows of Halloween.

So the next time you carve a pumpkin or don a costume, remember—you're not just participating in a fun, commercial holiday. You're engaging in rituals that have been passed down for millennia, connecting you to the ancient past, to the forces of death and rebirth that the Celts honored every year. Halloween is more than candy and costumes—it's a night when the dead walk among the living, when the veil is thin, and when we are reminded of the inevitable cycle of life and death that governs us all. Embrace it, because the dark side of Halloween is where its true power lies.

~ 4 ~

BELTANE – FIRE, FERTILITY, AND THE MAYPOLE

If you think modern celebrations of spring are all about pastel colors, flower crowns, and dancing around the Maypole, then you're only seeing the sanitized version of what used to be one of the wildest, most primal festivals in the pagan calendar. Beltane, celebrated on May 1st, marks the halfway point between the spring equinox and the summer solstice. It's a festival that's all about fire, fertility, and f***ing—yes, literally.

Beltane was the ancient Celts' celebration of the blossoming of life, a time to honor fertility, the return of abundance, and the untamed forces of nature. But unlike Easter's subtle fertility symbols of eggs and rabbits, Beltane wasn't trying to be discreet about it. This festival was about sex, fire, and life in its rawest forms. Beltane was a celebration of the Earth's awakening, a ritualistic unleashing of sexual energy, and a time to honor the powerful union of the masculine and feminine forces that would ensure the fertility of the land.

So let's throw off the flower crowns and get to the real, primal essence of this ancient celebration—a time when bonfires lit up the night, communities came together for ritualistic sex and fertility rites, and the natural world was honored with a kind of abandon that would make modern society blush.

Beltane: The Sacred Fire Festival

Beltane, which translates to "bright fire," is one of the four major Celtic fire festivals. Along with Samhain, Imbolc, and Lughnasadh, Beltane marks a significant turning point in the Celtic year. Whereas Samhain signaled the beginning of the dark half of the year, Beltane is the festival of light, a celebration of life's return after the long, hard winter.

Fire, the most powerful element of the festival, represented both the literal and symbolic return of the sun's warmth. Bonfires were lit on hilltops and in the center of villages, roaring flames that symbolized purification, protection, and the spark of new life. These weren't just ordinary bonfires, though—these flames were sacred, lit in ritual to honor the gods and the earth itself.

The people would jump over the flames, driving their livestock between the fires to ensure fertility and protection for the coming year. Ashes from the fires were spread across the fields to bless the crops, a way of ensuring that the land would yield abundance in the months to come. This was raw elemental magic, the kind of act that connected the people directly to the forces of nature. In a world where survival was directly linked to the fertility of the land and animals, Beltane's fire rites weren't just symbolic—they were essential.

Sex and Fertility Rituals: Unleashing the Primal

If you think modern May Day celebrations are all fun and games, filled with wholesome dances around the Maypole, let me shatter that illusion for you. Beltane was about fertility in every sense of the word, and that meant engaging in ritualistic sex to honor the Earth's ability to produce life. The Maypole itself, that innocent-looking tall wooden pole decorated with ribbons, is a straight-up phallic symbol. Let's not pretend otherwise.

The Maypole dance, where men and women wove colorful ribbons around the pole, symbolized the union of the masculine and feminine forces—the meeting of Earth and Sky, God and Goddess, in a dance of fertility and creation. But that was just the beginning. As the night went on, the festival became a celebration of sexuality, fertility, and the raw life force that was needed to keep the Earth thriving.

In ancient times, Beltane was often marked by *handfasting*, a form of temporary marriage or sexual union that lasted for the duration of the festival—or, in some cases, for a full year and a day. These unions were meant to harness the energy of the Goddess and the God, channeling their creative forces into the land. Couples would slip away into the fields or forests to "bless" the land through their union, believing that their sexual energy would help ensure a bountiful harvest.

This wasn't viewed as scandalous—it was sacred. Sex was a way of connecting with the forces of nature, a ritual act that ensured the fertility of the land, the livestock, and the people themselves. It was raw, primal, and without shame—because, in the world of Beltane, sex was life. It was as essential as the sun's warmth or the rain that nourished the crops.

The Divine Union: God and Goddess Reborn

At the heart of Beltane is the sacred union of the divine masculine and feminine—the God and the Goddess. In Celtic mythology, this was the time when the Horned God, representing the masculine force of nature, joined with the Goddess in a sacred marriage.

The God, often symbolized by the Green Man or the Horned One, was seen as the personification of the wild, untamed forces of the natural world—the forests, the animals, and the male sexual energy.

The Goddess, on the other hand, represented the Earth itself—fertile, abundant, and life-giving. Beltane was the time when the Goddess, after emerging from her winter rest, became the Maiden once more, ready to unite with the God in a ritualistic act of creation. This divine union was reenacted in the physical world by the people themselves, through dances, rites, and yes, through sex.

The union of the God and Goddess wasn't just symbolic—it was believed to have real, tangible effects on the fertility of the land. By participating in the rituals of Beltane, the people were ensuring that the cycle of life would continue, that the crops would grow, and that the animals would thrive. The divine marriage was a cosmic dance, one that ensured the continued existence of life itself.

Christian Repression: Beltane's Transformation into May Day

Like with so many other pagan festivals, the Church didn't take kindly to the raw, primal nature of Beltane. Rituals celebrating fertility and sexual energy were seen as deeply sinful by the Christian authorities, who sought to repress these pagan practices and replace them with more "morally upright" celebrations.

But just like with Christmas and Easter, the Church couldn't completely wipe out Beltane. Instead, they did what they always did—they transformed it into something more palatable for Christian society. The Maypole, once a clear phallic symbol of fertility, was recast as a quaint village tradition. The sexual rites of Beltane were downplayed, and May Day became a time for wholesome, community gatherings. Children danced around the Maypole, and the sacred fires of Beltane became more symbolic than magical.

The Church tried to erase the wilder elements of Beltane, but the deeper meaning couldn't be fully eradicated. The traditions of Beltane were simply too powerful, too deeply ingrained in the people's relationship with the land, the seasons, and the cycles of life.

Modern May Day: The Sanitized Version of Beltane

Fast forward to today, and May Day is a far cry from the fire-lit, sex-charged festival that Beltane once was. Modern celebrations often focus on community picnics, maypole dances, and other quaint traditions, but the raw essence of Beltane has been stripped away. The wildness, the fire, the sexual energy—it's all been sanitized, made more palatable for a society that's uncomfortable with the primal forces that Beltane celebrates.

But even in its modern form, there are echoes of the past. The Maypole dance is still a symbolic representation of the union of masculine and feminine forces, even if most people don't realize it. The bonfires, though now more often replaced by fireworks or small, controlled fires, are still a nod to the ancient flames that once roared on Beltane night.

And for those who seek to reconnect with the true meaning of Beltane, the festival remains a powerful time to honor the Earth, the forces of fertility, and the wild energy of life itself. Beltane is about celebrating the raw, creative forces that drive the cycle of life. It's about embracing the natural world in all its messy, beautiful, sexual, and life-giving glory.

Conclusion: Reclaiming the Fire and Fertility of Beltane

Beltane is one of the most primal, powerful celebrations of the ancient world, a festival that honors the forces of life and fertility in their rawest forms. It's a time when fire blazes, when sexuality is sacred, and when the Earth is at its most fertile. And while modern society has tried to sanitize and repress the wilder elements of this ancient festival, the spirit of Beltane is still very much alive.

Beneath the ribbons and flowers of modern May Day lies a much older, much deeper tradition—one that celebrates the sacred union of masculine and feminine, the fire of creation, and the power of life itself. So whether you're dancing around the Maypole or lighting a bonfire in the dead of night, remember that Beltane is about more than just the return of spring—it's about the raw, untamed forces of life that drive us all. And no matter how much society tries to repress it, that energy will always rise, just like the flames of Beltane's sacred fire.

~ 5 ~

LUPERCALIA – BLOOD, LUST, AND VALENTINE'S DAY

Now it's time to turn our attention to the blood-soaked, sex-drenched festival that eventually became *Valentine's Day*. You might think of February 14th as a sweet, romantic holiday filled with roses, heart-shaped chocolates, and candlelit dinners, but the real story is far darker and way more primal. Before it was all about cards and Cupid, Valentine's Day had its roots in *Lupercalia*, a wild Roman festival dedicated to fertility, purification, and—let's be real—absolute chaos.

Lupercalia wasn't just about celebrating love—it was about celebrating lust, blood, and the raw, animalistic forces of sexuality. The Romans, never a people to shy away from extremes, marked the middle of February with a festival that involved ritualistic sacrifices, whipping women with strips of animal skin soaked in blood, and a complete upheaval of social norms. This wasn't your Hallmark version of love; this was a full-bodied, no-holds-barred, primal celebration of sex, fertility, and the carnal energy that fuels human life.

So, let's strip away the cutesy imagery of Valentine's Day and dive headfirst into the raw, bloody roots of one of the most misunderstood holidays on the calendar. Lupercalia wasn't about romance—it was about survival, power, and sex. And as we peel back the layers of time, you'll see that Valentine's Day is just a sanitized remnant of a festival that was once wild, fierce, and untamed.

Lupercalia: The Wild Roman Festival of Fertility

Celebrated from February 13th to 15th, Lupercalia was one of the most important festivals in ancient Rome. It honored Lupercus, the god of fertility, agriculture, and shepherds, as well as *Faunus*, a Roman god of the forest and flocks. But at its core, Lupercalia was a festival about *purification* and *fertility*—a time when the Romans sought to cleanse themselves of evil spirits and ensure the fertility of the land, animals, and people.

The festival was named after the *Lupercal*, a sacred cave on the Palatine Hill where, according to legend, the she-wolf (the *lupa*) suckled Romulus and Remus, the twin founders of Rome. The she-wolf, a symbol of wildness and primal power, became central to the imagery of Lupercalia. The festival wasn't just about celebrating Rome's mythological origins; it was about reconnecting with the primal, animalistic forces that drove life and creation.

Lupercalia began with a series of rituals that were as bloody as they were symbolic. The festival kicked off with the sacrifice of goats and a dog by the *Luperci*, a group of priests dedicated to the god Lupercus. The blood of the animals was considered sacred, representing both purification and the raw energy of life and death. Once the animals were sacrificed, the priests would anoint themselves with the blood, smearing it on their foreheads, then wiping it away with wool soaked in milk—another powerful symbol of life and nourishment.

After this bloody initiation, the Luperci would cut strips of goat hide—called *februa*—from the freshly sacrificed animals, and then things got *wild*.

Blood and Lust: The Whipping Ritual

If there's one thing that Lupercalia is remembered for, it's the ritual of whipping. Once the animal skins were cut, the Luperci would run naked—or nearly naked—through the streets of Rome, whipping anyone they came across with the strips of bloody hide. And here's the kicker—women *wanted* to be whipped. In fact, they lined up for it.

Why? Because being struck by the februa was believed to bestow fertility and ensure an easy childbirth. Women hoping to become pregnant—or those already with child—would willingly expose themselves to be struck by the blood-soaked strips of animal skin, believing that the raw energy of the sacrifice and the symbolic power of the animal's fertility would transfer to them. This wasn't just a masochistic tradition; it was a deeply rooted belief in the power of blood and ritual to influence life and fertility.

This practice wasn't some fringe activity—it was central to the festival. The whipping ritual was a public display of the Romans' belief in the primal forces that governed fertility and reproduction. And while today we may see Valentine's Day as a time for tender, emotional love, Lupercalia was about something far more carnal: the raw, physical act of creation and the bloody rituals that went hand in hand with it.

Matchmaking and Sexual Freedom

Lupercalia wasn't just about purification and fertility; it was also about *sexual liberation.* As the festival progressed, the Roman social order was upended, and the strict societal norms that governed everyday life were temporarily thrown aside. Lupercalia offered a sanctioned period of chaos, where people were free to express their sexual desires without the usual restrictions of Roman morality.

One of the key aspects of Lupercalia was the *matchmaking lottery*. In this ritual, men and women would draw names from a jar, and whoever they were paired with would become their sexual partner for the duration of the festival—or longer, depending on how things worked out. These pairings weren't necessarily based on love or emotional connection; they were more about raw physicality, lust, and the celebration of the primal forces that drove human relationships.

In a society that was often rigid in its class distinctions and gender roles, Lupercalia was a rare moment when these rules were relaxed, and people were free to indulge their sexual desires without fear of judgment or retribution. The festival was a release valve for the tensions of everyday Roman life, a time when lust and passion were celebrated rather than suppressed.

But don't get it twisted—this wasn't some romantic interlude. Lupercalia was about sex, not love. It was about the power of the body, the drive to reproduce, and the belief that fertility and sexual energy were intertwined with the forces that governed life and death. It was a raw, untamed celebration of the body's primal urges, a far cry from the sanitized version of love that Valentine's Day has become.

The Transition to Valentine's Day: Christianity's Takeover

So, how did we get from blood-soaked goat hides and wild sexual freedom to Valentine's Day cards and heart-shaped chocolates? Like with most pagan festivals, the Christian church couldn't completely eradicate Lupercalia, so they did the next best thing—they co-opted it.

By the 5th century, Pope Gelasius I had had enough of the wild debauchery of Lupercalia. In an effort to "Christianize" the festival, he officially replaced Lupercalia with *St. Valentine's Day*, a feast day honoring the Christian martyr, St. Valentine. The story of St. Valentine is murky at best—there are multiple saints by that name, and the actual history behind the saint is vague and shrouded in legend.

The most common story is that St. Valentine was a priest who defied the Roman Emperor Claudius II by performing marriages for Christian couples in secret, against the emperor's orders. Claudius had banned marriages in an effort to build his army, believing that single men made better soldiers. Valentine, however, continued to marry couples in defiance of the law, and for this, he was executed on February 14th.

Valentine's Day was meant to shift the focus from the wild, carnal celebrations of Lupercalia to something more pious and focused on Christian love and martyrdom. But let's be real—the old festival never really went away. The sexual undertones of Lupercalia still pulse beneath the surface of Valentine's Day, even if they've been hidden under layers of commercialized romance and sentimentality.

Cupid: A Pagan God in Disguise

Let's not forget the mascot of Valentine's Day—*Cupid*. The cherubic, winged figure who flutters around shooting arrows into the hearts of lovers may seem harmless, but his origins are far from innocent. Cupid, known to the Romans as *Eros* to the Greeks, was the god of desire, erotic love, and passion. He wasn't the cutesy figure we see today; he was a powerful god who could inflame the hearts of both mortals and gods with uncontrollable lust.

In fact, in early depictions, Cupid was often portrayed as a mischievous and dangerous figure, capable of causing chaos by making people fall hopelessly in love—or lust—against their will. The arrows of Cupid didn't always bring tender feelings; sometimes they sparked fiery, destructive passions that could tear lives apart. In this way, Cupid represents the uncontrollable nature of desire—the way love and lust can sweep over us like a force of nature, overwhelming our senses and leaving us powerless in its wake.

So while modern Valentine's Day portrays Cupid as a benign, love-struck figure, his roots lie in the much older and darker mythology of desire and eroticism. Cupid, like the rest of Valentine's Day, has been sanitized for public consumption, but beneath his harmless exterior is the raw power of lust, the primal force that drove festivals like Lupercalia.

From Blood to Candy: The Commercialization of Valentine's Day

As the centuries wore on, Valentine's Day became increasingly detached from its darker, more primal origins. By the 19th century, it had transformed into a celebration of romantic love, with the first mass-produced Valentine's Day cards appearing in England in the 1840s. What was once a festival of blood, sacrifice, and sexual liberation had become a commercial holiday, a way to sell cards, flowers, and candy.

The deeper, darker elements of Lupercalia were scrubbed away, leaving only the superficial trappings of "love" and "romance." Today, Valentine's Day is celebrated around the world as a day of courtship, gift-giving, and sentimental expressions of love. But the wild, untamed energy of Lupercalia—the whipping, the blood, the animal sacrifice—has been almost entirely erased, hidden beneath the layers of consumer culture and Christian morality.

But if you look closely, you can still see the traces of Lupercalia in modern Valentine's Day. The focus on fertility, the pairing off of couples, the underlying themes of lust and desire—all of these are remnants of the ancient festival that celebrated the primal forces of life and creation. The passion that Valentine's Day claims to celebrate is, in fact, the same energy that fueled Lupercalia—only now it's wrapped in pink ribbons and sold for $19.99 at your local drugstore.

Conclusion: Reclaiming the Raw Power of Love and Lust

Valentine's Day may have evolved into a sugary, commercialized celebration of love, but its roots in Lupercalia remind us that love and lust are far more complex—and far more primal—than what we see on the surface. Lupercalia was a festival that celebrated the raw, untamed forces of desire, fertility, and creation. It was a time of blood and passion, a celebration of life's most primal instincts.

Today, Valentine's Day has lost much of that raw power, but the energy of Lupercalia still pulses beneath the surface. Love and lust, after all, are not neat and tidy emotions—they are wild, uncontrollable forces that drive us, just as they drove the Romans to whip their lovers with blood-soaked hides.

So the next time you buy a Valentine's Day card or give your partner a box of chocolates, remember that you're participating in a ritual that has far deeper, darker roots than you might think. Valentine's Day isn't just about love—it's about the wild, fiery energy of desire, the blood that pumps through our veins, and the primal forces that make us human. And if you really want to honor the spirit of Lupercalia, maybe skip the roses and reach for something a little more... primal.

6

THANKSGIVING – BLOOD, SACRIFICE, AND THE HARVEST

When you think of Thanksgiving, what comes to mind? A picturesque autumn scene, a table overflowing with food, family gathered around to express gratitude, and a roast turkey as the centerpiece? It's all so warm, wholesome, and quintessentially American, right? But that image, wrapped up in feel-good mythology about pilgrims and Native Americans sharing a peaceful meal, is nothing more than a whitewashed fantasy. The truth about Thanksgiving—its real roots—are far more ancient, blood-soaked, and primal.

Thanksgiving is just one of the many harvest festivals that humans have been celebrating for millennia. Long before the settlers landed on Plymouth Rock, long before anyone gave thanks for a bountiful harvest by gathering with family, ancient cultures were honoring the harvest with blood sacrifices, offerings to the gods, and wild, ritualistic feasts. In these ancient harvest festivals, survival wasn't guaranteed, and giving thanks wasn't about polite gratitude—it was about ensuring that the forces of nature were kept in balance, that the gods were appeased, and that the land would continue to provide.

Beneath the veneer of turkey, stuffing, and pie lies a far older and more savage truth: Thanksgiving, like all harvest festivals, is rooted in humanity's oldest fears and desires—the desperate need to survive winter, the reverence for the land, and the belief that blood, death, and sacrifice were necessary to ensure life. The cozy, sanitized version of Thanksgiving we know today is just a shadow of the ancient rites that once honored the raw forces of life and death.

So let's strip away the myth of Thanksgiving and get to the truth—a truth soaked in blood, sacrifice, and the primal need to survive.

The Ancient Harvest Festivals: Life and Death in Balance

Before we can understand the roots of Thanksgiving, we need to look at the ancient harvest festivals that predate it. Across the world, from Mesopotamia to Egypt to Europe, harvest time was celebrated with elaborate festivals that honored the gods of agriculture, fertility, and the land itself. These festivals were a time to give thanks, yes, but they were also a time of sacrifice—because the ancient world understood one brutal truth: you had to give in order to receive.

Take, for example, the ancient Greeks and their *Thesmophoria*, a three-day festival in honor of Demeter, the goddess of the harvest and fertility. Women would gather for rites that involved fasting, offerings, and sacrifices to ensure the fertility of the land. The Romans had their own version, *Ceres' Day*, dedicated to their version of the harvest goddess, Ceres. Both festivals were as much about honoring the forces of nature as they were about ensuring that those forces would continue to provide.

And these weren't peaceful, sanitized events. **Blood sacrifices were often the main course**—animals, and sometimes even humans, were sacrificed to the gods as offerings of life to ensure that the harvest would come again. In ancient Egypt, farmers would make offerings to *Osiris*, the god of death and rebirth, to ensure the fertility of the Nile. Human sacrifices weren't unheard of, and the blood of the sacrificed would be seen as a way to appease the gods and renew the cycle of life and death.

Even the Celts had their own harvest festival, *Lughnasadh*, celebrated on August 1st. This was a time to honor Lugh, the god of the sun, and to give thanks for the first fruits of the harvest. Like the other ancient cultures, the Celts understood that the land required offerings, often in the form of animal sacrifices, to maintain balance between life and death. Blood was spilled to ensure the harvest would continue.

And let's not forget the Aztecs, whose agricultural festivals took human sacrifice to an entirely different level. To honor *Tlaloc*, the god of rain and fertility, the Aztecs would offer the hearts of captured slaves and warriors. These offerings were believed to bring rain and ensure the fertility of the crops. In a brutal yet undeniable way, the ancient world believed that life could only continue if death was offered in exchange.

These festivals weren't just about gratitude—they were about survival. If the crops failed, people starved. Winter was coming, and it was unforgiving. The ancients understood that the cycle of life and death needed to be respected, and that meant making sacrifices, both literal and symbolic, to the forces of nature and the gods that controlled them.

The First Thanksgiving: The Myth of Pilgrims and Peace

Fast forward to the 17th century, when the story of the first Thanksgiving was born. The popular version goes like this: In 1621, the Pilgrims, after enduring a harsh winter and barely surviving, gathered with the Wampanoag Native Americans to celebrate a successful harvest. The two groups supposedly shared a peaceful meal, and everyone gave thanks for their survival and the bounty of the land.

It's a beautiful story, but it's not the full truth. The idea that the first Thanksgiving was a peaceful, harmonious feast between Pilgrims and Native Americans is a myth that was constructed long after the fact, conveniently ignoring the bloody history of colonialism, violence, and land theft that would follow.

In reality, the Pilgrims were not the gentle, peaceful settlers we've been taught to imagine. They were religious zealots, driven by a desire to carve out a new world based on their strict Puritan beliefs. The Wampanoag, who did indeed share food with the Pilgrims, were not meeting as equals in a peaceful celebration—they were ensuring their own survival in the face of growing threats from European settlers. The relationship between Native Americans and settlers was complex, fraught with tension, violence, and betrayal. What followed the "first Thanksgiving" was a centuries-long campaign of genocide, displacement, and colonization of Native peoples.

So while the myth of the first Thanksgiving paints a picture of unity and gratitude, the truth is far more complicated—and far bloodier.

The Real Roots of Thanksgiving: Sacrifice and Survival

So where does Thanksgiving truly come from? It's easy to point to the Pilgrims and their meal with the Wampanoag, but the real roots of Thanksgiving lie in those ancient harvest festivals, where the connection between life and death was understood in its rawest form. The Pilgrims themselves were well aware of these traditions, as many of them came from cultures that still practiced harvest festivals, albeit in Christianized forms.

In Europe, before the Puritans left for the New World, the harvest was marked by Christianized versions of the ancient pagan festivals. In England, there was *Harvest Home*, a festival that included feasting, drinking, and giving thanks for the successful gathering of crops. It was a time to celebrate, but also a time to acknowledge the precariousness of life—after all, if the harvest failed, winter would be brutal.

The Puritans, though deeply religious and determined to build a new life based on strict Christian principles, still carried with them the echoes of these older traditions. When they gathered to give thanks for their survival and the bounty of the land in 1621, they were engaging in an ancient ritual that stretched back thousands of years—a ritual of gratitude, but also one of survival.

The real story of Thanksgiving is not one of peaceful meals and polite gratitude. It's a story of sacrifice, of blood and death given in exchange for life. The Pilgrims gave thanks because they had survived—barely. They gave thanks because they had not starved to death, and because the land had provided. But beneath their prayers of gratitude lay the same primal truth that the ancient world understood: survival is not guaranteed, and sometimes, you have to offer life to ensure it.

Sacrifice and Blood: The Forgotten Element of Thanksgiving

It's important to remember that in the ancient world, giving thanks to the gods wasn't just about saying a prayer or offering a polite meal. It was about blood. The idea of sacrifice—whether animal or human—was central to the harvest festivals. Blood was seen as a life force, a sacred substance that connected the living to the gods. By offering blood, people believed they were maintaining the delicate balance between life and death, ensuring that the land would continue to provide.

In a way, the traditional Thanksgiving turkey is a sanitized version of these older, bloodier sacrifices. The turkey, once killed and prepared for the feast, is a symbolic stand-in for the animals (or people) who were sacrificed in ancient times to ensure the fertility of the land. It's a far cry from the human hearts offered up to Tlaloc or the blood spilled in honor of Demeter, but the essence remains: a life is given so that life may continue.

Of course, we don't think of it that way anymore. Modern Thanksgiving has become a holiday focused on family, food, and gratitude. The deeper, darker elements of sacrifice and survival have been scrubbed away, replaced by Norman Rockwell images of families gathered around a table. But that sanitized version of Thanksgiving doesn't erase its roots in the ancient traditions of blood and sacrifice.

The Indigenous Perspective: Erasing the Real Story

One of the most glaring omissions in the traditional Thanksgiving narrative is the experience of the Native American peoples who were systematically displaced, slaughtered, and stripped of their lands in the years following the arrival of the Pilgrims. While we're told to give thanks for the bounty of the land, we conveniently forget that this land was stolen, often through acts of extreme violence and betrayal.

For Native Americans, Thanksgiving isn't a celebration of peace and unity—it's a reminder of the genocide that followed. The Wampanoag people, who were present at the first Thanksgiving, would soon see their population decimated by disease, war, and displacement. The arrival of European settlers marked the beginning of the end for many indigenous peoples, whose way of life was irrevocably changed by colonization.

So while we sit around the table and give thanks for what we have, it's important to remember what was taken. The myth of Thanksgiving as a peaceful, harmonious celebration erases the brutal history of colonialism that followed. The blood sacrifices of the ancient world may be forgotten, but the blood of Native peoples stains the land we now claim as our own.

Conclusion: The Dark Side of Gratitude

Thanksgiving, as we celebrate it today, is a shadow of its former self. Beneath the turkey, the stuffing, and the family gatherings lies a far older tradition—one rooted in blood, sacrifice, and the desperate need to survive. The ancient harvest festivals that gave rise to Thanksgiving were brutal, bloody affairs, where life and death were balanced on a knife's edge, and the forces of nature were honored with sacrifices to ensure the continuation of life.

And while the modern version of Thanksgiving may seem wholesome and peaceful, the truth is far more complicated. Thanksgiving's roots lie in the ancient understanding that survival is never guaranteed, that the land must be respected, and that life often requires sacrifice. It's a reminder of our connection to the earth, to the cycles of life and death, and to the bloody history that has shaped the world we live in.

So when you sit down to your Thanksgiving meal, remember that you're participating in a ritual as old as humanity itself—a ritual that honors life, but also acknowledges the power of death. Thanksgiving isn't just about gratitude; it's about survival, sacrifice, and the ancient truth that nothing comes without a cost.

7

NEW YEAR'S EVE – THE DARK HISTORY OF DEATH

When you think of New Year's Eve, what comes to mind? Glitzy parties, fireworks, champagne toasts at midnight, and the collective hope that the new year will bring better things than the last. It's a celebration marked by optimism, a time to leave behind the old and welcome the new. But before it became a night of glittery celebration, New Year's Eve—like many of our modern holidays—was born out of ancient, dark rituals focused on death, rebirth, and the inevitable cycle of time. It wasn't about resolutions or new beginnings in the way we think of them today—it was about confronting the dark forces that ruled over life and death, and appeasing the gods who controlled time itself.

New Year's Eve is a modern interpretation of an ancient festival that was far more serious, far more primal, and rooted in the recognition that time was a force beyond human control. To the ancient world, time wasn't just a passive thing that passed by unnoticed—it was a powerful, often destructive force that brought with it the inevitability of death and the need for renewal. The cycle of time was both feared and revered, and the transition from one year to the next was a dangerous, liminal space where the boundaries between the human world and the supernatural thinned.

In this chapter, we'll strip away the party hats and confetti to uncover the dark, ancient roots of New Year's Eve. From the time-bending rituals of the Babylonians to the orgiastic chaos of the Romans' *Kalends*, we'll explore how the ancients viewed the end of the year as a time of death, a reckoning with the old before the world could be reborn into something new.

Babylonian New Year: The Cycle of Death and Rebirth

Let's start by going back to ancient Babylon, one of the first civilizations to mark the beginning of a new year with an elaborate festival. The Babylonian New Year, known as *Akitu*, was celebrated in March during the spring equinox—not January—because it was seen as the natural time for renewal. But unlike modern New Year's celebrations, *Akitu* wasn't just about celebrating; it was about survival.

The Babylonians believed that the gods, especially Marduk, the god of creation and chaos, determined the fate of the world at the start of each new year. The festival of *Akitu* was a way to symbolically reenact the creation of the universe, with rituals that acknowledged the chaotic forces of death and destruction. In Babylonian mythology, the world had been created out of chaos, and every year, that chaos threatened to return. The festival was a time to restore order to the world, to ensure that life would continue and that the gods wouldn't allow the world to fall back into chaos.

During *Akitu*, the king would symbolically die and be reborn as part of the ritual, representing the death of the old year and the rebirth of the new one. He would be stripped of his royal garments, humiliated, and ritually beaten to symbolize his submission to the gods. Only after this symbolic death could the king be restored to power, representing the renewal of life and the world's survival for another year.

These rituals reflected a deep understanding of the cyclical nature of time: death followed life, and destruction preceded renewal. The new year wasn't just a time for celebration—it was a time to confront the forces of death and chaos head-on, to ensure that the cycle could begin again.

Roman Kalends: Saturnalia's Wild Successor

While the Babylonians celebrated their New Year in spring, the Romans shifted the calendar to align with the winter solstice and eventually settled on January 1st as the start of the new year. But before January 1st became the official date, the Romans had a different way of marking the end of the year, and it was a far cry from the civilized parties of today.

The Roman *Kalends*—the first day of each month—was originally tied to the new moon and was a time of great importance. But it was the *Kalends of January* that marked the official new year, and it was a chaotic, riotous celebration. Coming on the heels of the infamous festival of *Saturnalia*, the Roman New Year was a time of excess, debauchery, and wild behavior. It was a period of *total upheaval*, much like Saturnalia, where the normal rules of society were suspended, and people were free to indulge in behavior that was normally forbidden.

In the spirit of Saturnalia's role reversal, during the *Kalends*, slaves were allowed to insult their masters, children were given temporary control over adults, and social hierarchies were turned upside down. The Roman people believed that the chaos and excess of the *Kalends* were necessary to bring balance to the universe—to allow the chaotic forces to reign temporarily so that order could be restored in the new year. Like the Babylonians, the Romans understood that before a new cycle could begin, the old world had to be symbolically destroyed.

One of the most important figures during the Roman New Year celebrations was *Janus*, the god of time, beginnings, and transitions. Janus was depicted with two faces—one looking forward into the future, and the other looking backward into the past. He was the perfect symbol of the New Year, a time when people were caught between the old and the new, between death and renewal.

The Romans believed that Janus ruled over the transition from one year to the next and that his favor was essential to ensuring a prosperous new year. Offerings were made to Janus, and prayers were offered to ensure that the new year would be filled with good fortune, protection, and renewal.

But let's not forget—the *Kalends* were still rooted in *Saturnalia's* spirit of wild abandon. Drinking, orgies, and gambling were rampant, and the normally strict Roman social order was temporarily dissolved. It was a time when people acted out their desires and gave in to the chaos, knowing that once the new year officially began, order would return, and the gods would have been appeased.

The Christian Shift: Rebranding the New Year

As Christianity spread through the Roman Empire, the church worked hard to suppress the wild, chaotic elements of the pagan New Year's celebrations. The church fathers saw the debauchery of the *Kalends* as sinful, and the worship of Janus was replaced by more Christian-friendly rituals. The Roman Catholic Church, always adept at repurposing pagan festivals, began to shift the focus of the New Year toward solemn reflection and prayer, rather than debauchery and chaos. The church rebranded January 1st as the Feast of the Circumcision of Jesus, a holy day that was supposed to replace the wild celebrations dedicated to Janus and the unrestrained revelry of the *Kalends*.

But, as with so many other ancient festivals, the spirit of the old ways never fully disappeared. Despite the church's attempts to Christianize the new year, many of the pagan traditions remained in the collective consciousness. People still celebrated with feasting, drinking, and making noise to ward off evil spirits—a nod to the ancient belief that the new year was a dangerous time when the veil between worlds was thin, and supernatural forces could easily slip into the human realm.

The idea of time as a powerful, dangerous force didn't vanish either. Even as Christianity attempted to impose a more linear, controlled view of time and history, the primal, cyclical understanding of time as a force of destruction and renewal persisted. The church may have replaced Janus with Jesus, but the fear and reverence for the passage of time—along with the need to mark its transition—was too deeply embedded in human culture to be erased.

Medieval New Year's: Darkness and Superstition

As the medieval period began, New Year's celebrations were still heavily influenced by the dark, superstitious beliefs of earlier times. While the official church-sanctioned holiday was centered on prayer and reflection, the common people continued to observe many of the older pagan customs, blending them with Christian practices.

Medieval Europeans believed that the transition from the old year to the new was a dangerous time when evil spirits, ghosts, and witches roamed freely. The idea of the *thinning of the veil* between worlds wasn't confined to Halloween or Samhain; it applied to New Year's Eve as well. As the clock struck midnight, people would make loud noises—banging pots, ringing bells, and setting off firecrackers—to scare away evil spirits and prevent them from entering the new year. This custom of "making noise" to protect against supernatural forces is still echoed in our modern-day fireworks displays and raucous New Year's Eve parties.

In addition to protecting against evil spirits, medieval people were deeply concerned with omens and portents during the New Year. The first person to cross your threshold after midnight was believed to be especially important, as their character would determine the fortune of your household for the entire year. This tradition, known as "first-footing," is still practiced in some cultures today, particularly in Scotland, where it's believed that a dark-haired man entering your home first will bring good luck, while a fair-haired person could signal disaster.

Medieval New Year's Eve was also a time of intense superstition regarding death. It was believed that if a person died during the last few hours of the old year or the first hours of the new, their soul was trapped in limbo, caught between the two worlds. This belief reinforced the idea that New Year's Eve was a liminal time—a space where the boundaries between life and death, past and future, were blurred, and anything could happen.

New Year's Resolutions: A Pagan Legacy

One of the most enduring traditions associated with New Year's Eve is the practice of making resolutions. Today, we think of resolutions as promises to ourselves—goals to lose weight, quit smoking, save more money, or generally become better versions of ourselves. But the roots of this tradition are deeply pagan, and they reflect the same themes of renewal, death, and rebirth that have always been central to New Year's celebrations.

The ancient Babylonians are credited with starting the tradition of New Year's resolutions. During the *Akitu* festival, they would make promises to the gods to repay their debts and return borrowed objects, hoping to earn favor for the coming year. These resolutions weren't just personal goals—they were spiritual obligations, meant to cleanse the individual of their past wrongs and ensure divine protection.

The Romans, too, made resolutions during the *Kalends*. They would offer sacrifices to Janus and make promises to improve their behavior in the new year, seeking to win his favor and avoid his wrath. This idea of self-improvement as a form of spiritual purification was central to the Roman understanding of the New Year—a time when the slate was wiped clean, and people could begin again.

As Christianity spread, the concept of New Year's resolutions took on a more religious tone, with believers vowing to repent for their sins and live more pious lives in the coming year. The focus shifted from pleasing the gods to pleasing the Christian God, but the underlying idea remained the same: the old year had to die, and with it, the mistakes of the past, so that the new year could bring renewal and redemption.

Today, our resolutions may be less about spiritual purity and more about self-improvement, but the core of the tradition is still

rooted in the ancient belief that the new year is a time for transformation, a time to shed the old and embrace the new.

New Year's Eve Today: Echoes of the Past

So here we are, in the modern world, where New Year's Eve is
celebrated with fireworks, countdowns, champagne, and parties
that stretch well past midnight. But even in our most modern celebrations, we can still see the echoes of the ancient rituals that once
dominated this time of year.

The fireworks that light up the sky are our modern version of
the noise-making rituals designed to ward off evil spirits. The collective countdown to midnight is a holdover from the liminal nature of the New Year—the recognition that we are passing through
a dangerous, uncertain time when the past and future collide, and
the forces of chaos are at their strongest. And the idea of "starting
fresh," of making resolutions and leaving behind the old year, is a
direct descendant of the ancient belief in death and rebirth as part
of the natural cycle of time.

But here's the thing—New Year's Eve, even today, still carries
with it a sense of danger and unpredictability. Think about how
many people describe New Year's Eve as a night when "anything
can happen." There's a reason why it's often associated with wild
parties, reckless behavior, and moments of uncharacteristic bold-
ness. The energy of the night—the sense that time itself is in
flux—creates an atmosphere where the normal rules don't apply.
It's a night when we give ourselves permission to indulge, to break
free from our routines, to act out in ways we might not the rest of
the year.

This is the same energy that fueled the wild festivals of the *Kalends* and Saturnalia, the same chaotic force that the Babylonians feared when they reenacted the creation of the universe. New Year's Eve is a night of transition, and transitions are always dangerous, always liminal. It's a night when we face the unknown, when we teeter on the edge of the future, not knowing what's to come.

Conclusion: Embracing the Chaos of New Year's

New Year's Eve, for all its modern glitz and glamour, is still a night steeped in ancient magic, danger, and the powerful forces of death and rebirth. Beneath the fireworks and the champagne toasts lies the recognition that time itself is something to be feared, something that cannot be controlled. The passage from one year to the next is not just a simple turning of the calendar—it's a moment when we confront the inevitability of time's march forward, when we acknowledge the death of the old and the uncertain birth of the new.

The ancient world understood this far better than we do today. To them, the New Year was a time of ritualistic reckoning, a time to appease the gods, to make sacrifices, and to ensure that the chaos of the past year wouldn't carry over into the new one. Today, we may not make blood sacrifices or offer prayers to Janus, but the energy of the night is still there, pulsing beneath the surface.

So when you raise your glass at midnight, when you make your resolutions or kiss someone under the fireworks, remember that you are participating in a ritual that is far older, far deeper, and far darker than you may realize. New Year's Eve is a celebration of life and death, of chaos and renewal, and it is a night when time itself stands still, if only for a moment, before the future rushes in.

As the clock strikes midnight, embrace the chaos, honor the past, and prepare for the inevitable rebirth of the new year. Because no matter how much we try to control it, time is always more powerful than we are—and New Year's Eve is the night when we are forced to confront that truth.

Conclusion: The Blood of the Ancients Flows On

What do you think you're really celebrating when you sit down for Christmas dinner, hide Easter eggs in the backyard, or set off fireworks on New Year's Eve? Is it the sanitized version of history that's been spoon-fed to you since childhood—the fairy tales of saints, saviors, and holiday cheer? Or is it something far older, far darker, and far more powerful, buried beneath centuries of religious control, capitalism, and cultural whitewashing?

The truth is, the holidays we celebrate today are little more than echoes of the raw, primal festivals of our ancestors. These were not polite, sanitized celebrations. They were wild, blood-soaked rituals filled with sex, sacrifice, and magic. They weren't about religion as we know it today—they were about survival. They were about the eternal cycles of life and death, fertility and decay, light and darkness. They were about confronting the unknown forces that ruled the natural world and seeking favor from the gods, spirits, and unseen powers that held human lives in their hands.

For thousands of years, our ancestors celebrated the turning of the seasons, the balance of the elements, and the forces of the universe with rituals that were direct, physical, and deeply connected to the earth. These were not "holidays" in the sense that we understand them today—they were life-or-death affairs, times when the veil between the worlds was thin and the survival of the tribe, the village, or the community depended on making the right sacrifices and honoring the right gods.

The Theft and Rebranding of Pagan Rituals

As we've seen throughout this book, the story of our modern holidays is one of theft, rebranding, and sanitization. Christianity, as it spread across Europe and beyond, couldn't wipe out the deep, ancient traditions of pagan cultures. Instead, it did what it always does—it co-opted them. It took the raw, visceral power of these festivals and buried them under layers of doctrine, moral superiority, and myth.

Christmas was ripped from the wild, untamed roots of Yule and Saturnalia, festivals that celebrated the rebirth of the sun and the reversal of social norms. Easter was carved out of the blood-soaked fertility rites of Ishtar and Ostara, where the resurrection of life was marked by sacrifices to goddesses of sex and death. Halloween, with all its commercialized costumes and candy, is still a remnant of Samhain, a festival of death where the spirits of the dead walked the earth and demanded respect. And Valentine's Day? Forget the romantic gestures and cute Cupid—its true origins lie in the primal, sexual chaos of Lupercalia, a festival where fertility was fueled by blood, lust, and the tearing apart of social norms.

These holidays were never meant to be tamed. They were raw, primal acts of ritual and magic, designed to connect humans to the forces of nature in ways that were direct, physical, and dangerous. They weren't about gratitude, family gatherings, or exchanging gifts—they were about survival, fertility, and confronting the terrifying, uncontrollable forces of the universe.

The Ancient Magic Still Pulses Beneath the Surface

But here's the thing: no matter how much Christianity, capitalism, or modern society tries to bury these ancient festivals under a pile of greeting cards and consumerism, the raw energy of those old rituals still pulses beneath the surface. It's still there, waiting to be uncovered, acknowledged, and reclaimed.

When you light a Christmas tree, you're invoking the same primal energy that pagans once honored with fire and offerings to the sun god. When you paint Easter eggs or hide them in the yard, you're channeling the ancient fertility rites of goddesses who demanded blood and life to ensure the world's survival. When you dress up in a Halloween costume, you're reenacting a tradition meant to protect you from the spirits of the dead who walk the earth on Samhain night. And when you toast to the new year, making resolutions you'll never keep, you're stepping into the same dangerous, liminal space that the Romans feared during their wild celebrations of the *Kalends*, where the forces of chaos were unleashed before order could be restored.

These traditions aren't just ancient—they're eternal. They represent the most fundamental forces of the universe: creation, destruction, birth, death, light, darkness, and the endless cycle that governs all life. The modern world may have tried to domesticate them, but their power is still there, lying dormant, waiting for those who are brave enough to see beyond the surface.

Reclaiming the Primal Power of the Past

So, what do we do with this knowledge? Do we continue to blindly celebrate the hollow, commercialized versions of these ancient festivals, or do we reclaim the raw power that they once held? That's up to you.

Understanding the true origins of these holidays doesn't mean rejecting them—it means seeing them for what they really are. It means recognizing that when you gather with family for Christmas, Easter, or Thanksgiving, you're participating in rituals that stretch back thousands of years, to a time when life and death were far closer, far more intertwined, and far more dangerous. It means acknowledging that the gods, goddesses, spirits, and primal forces that once demanded blood and sacrifice still linger beneath the surface of our modern world, waiting for us to remember them.

Reclaiming these festivals means reconnecting with the earth, with the cycles of nature, and with the raw, untamed forces that our ancestors honored with fire, sex, and blood. It means understanding that the holidays we celebrate today are echoes of something far more powerful, something that can't be controlled or sanitized. It means remembering that, beneath the tinsel and the turkey, the ancient magic of these festivals is still alive, still pulsing through the earth, still calling to those who are willing to listen.

The blood of the ancients still flows through these holidays. And now that you know the truth, it's up to you to decide how you'll honor it.

The Final Truth: Nothing Is Lost, Only Buried

In the end, the truth about modern holidays is simple: nothing is ever truly lost. The gods of old are still with us. The primal forces of life, death, fertility, and renewal are still woven into the fabric of our celebrations, no matter how much we try to cover them up with fairy tales and consumerism.

As you celebrate the holidays going forward, I challenge you to look beneath the surface. See the echoes of the blood sacrifices, the sexual rites, the fire rituals, and the deep connection to the earth that these festivals once represented. Reclaim that power. Honor the ancient forces. Because the truth is, the blood of the ancients is still there, pulsing just beneath the surface of every holiday, waiting for you to awaken it.

And once you do, you'll never see these celebrations the same way again.

Definitions

Paganism: A broad term used to describe ancient religions and spiritual practices that existed before the rise of Christianity, often focused on the worship of nature, gods, and goddesses tied to the earth, seasons, fertility, and the cycles of life and death.

Yule: A winter solstice festival celebrated by the ancient Germanic and Norse peoples, marking the longest night of the year and the rebirth of the sun. Yule traditions, such as the Yule log and the Christmas tree, heavily influenced modern Christmas celebrations.

Saturnalia: An ancient Roman festival held in December to honor Saturn, the god of agriculture and time. Known for its chaos and role reversals, it involved feasting, gift-giving, and the temporary overturning of social hierarchies, influencing modern Christmas and New Year traditions.

Samhain: A Celtic festival marking the end of the harvest season and the beginning of winter, celebrated on October 31st. Samhain was believed to be a time when the veil between the living and the dead was thin, allowing spirits to walk among the living. Modern Halloween is rooted in Samhain's customs and rituals.

Beltane: A fire festival celebrated on May 1st in honor of fertility, the blossoming of life, and the union of the masculine and feminine forces. Beltane rituals, such as dancing around the Maypole and bonfires, were designed to ensure fertility and abundance for the coming year.

Lupercalia: An ancient Roman fertility festival celebrated in mid-February, marked by the sacrifice of goats and dogs, the use of their skins in rituals to promote fertility, and wild behavior. Lupercalia eventually evolved into what we now know as Valentine's Day.

Harvest Festivals: Celebrations marking the end of the growing season, common in ancient cultures around the world. These festivals often involved offerings and sacrifices to the gods of agriculture and fertility to ensure a successful harvest in the future.

Human Sacrifice: A practice in many ancient cultures where human lives were offered to gods as part of religious rituals. These sacrifices were believed to appease the gods, ensure the fertility of the land, or guarantee survival during difficult times, such as winter or drought.

The Veil: A metaphorical barrier between the physical world and the spiritual or supernatural world, often believed to be thin during specific times of the year, such as Samhain (Halloween) or New Year's Eve. When the veil is thin, communication with the dead or otherworldly forces is thought to be possible.

Fertility Rites: Rituals designed to ensure the fertility of the land, animals, and people. Common in many ancient religions, these rites often involved sexual symbolism, offerings, and sometimes sacrifices to ensure abundance and the continuation of life.

Bonfire: A large, ceremonial fire used in many pagan rituals, especially during festivals like Beltane and Samhain. Bonfires were believed to purify, protect, and invite the forces of life, such as the sun, to return after the darkness of winter.

Ishtar: The Mesopotamian goddess of love, war, fertility, and sex. Known by different names in various cultures, such as Inanna or

Astarte, Ishtar's worship and fertility rites influenced the modern celebration of Easter.

Ostara: A spring equinox festival in ancient Germanic paganism, honoring the goddess of dawn and fertility. Ostara's symbols, such as eggs and rabbits, were adopted into modern Easter traditions.

Akitu: The ancient Babylonian New Year festival, celebrated in spring. It involved a symbolic reenactment of creation and the king's ritual death and rebirth, marking the end of chaos and the renewal of life.

First-Footing: A tradition that originated in Scotland and other parts of the UK, where the first person to enter a home after midnight on New Year's Eve was believed to bring good or bad luck for the coming year. Dark-haired visitors were seen as lucky, while light-haired ones were seen as a bad omen.

Handfasting: A form of pagan or pre-Christian wedding or betrothal, often performed during festivals like Beltane. It was a binding ritual that symbolized the union of two people, often for a year and a day, before the commitment was made permanent.

Maypole: A tall pole, often decorated with ribbons and flowers, used in May Day and Beltane celebrations. It is a phallic symbol representing fertility, and the dance around the Maypole symbolizes the intertwining of masculine and feminine energies.

The Wild Hunt: A supernatural phenomenon in European folklore, often associated with the god Odin. It involves a ghostly procession or hunt of spirits, deities, or the dead riding across the sky, typically during the winter or Yule season. Witnessing the Wild Hunt was believed to be a bad omen.

Janus: The Roman god of beginnings, transitions, and time, depicted with two faces—one looking to the past, and one to the future. He was central to Roman New Year's celebrations (the *Kalends*) and symbolizes the liminal space between the old and new year.

Kalends: The first day of each month in the Roman calendar, but most importantly, the *Kalends of January*, which marked the beginning of the new year. It was celebrated with chaotic festivities, and offerings were made to Janus to ensure a prosperous new year.

Dies Natalis Solis Invicti: "The Birthday of the Unconquered Sun," a Roman festival celebrated on December 25th, in honor of the sun god Sol. This celebration coincided with the winter solstice and heavily influenced the Christian choice of December 25th as the date for Christmas.

Human-Animal Hybrids in Ritual: Representations or symbolic use of human-animal hybrids, often seen in ancient fertility and sacrificial rituals. The wearing of animal skins and masks, like in Lupercalia, allowed participants to invoke or embody the primal powers of fertility and nature.

Sovereignty of the Land: An ancient belief that the fertility and abundance of the land depended on the proper rituals, sacrifices, and respect given to the gods, goddesses, and nature spirits. Without these rituals, it was believed that the land would become barren, and people would starve.

Thinning of the Veil: A belief in many ancient cultures that certain times of the year, such as Samhain or New Year's Eve, saw the boundary between the physical world and the spiritual world weaken, allowing spirits and other supernatural forces to cross over and interact with the living.

Fire Jumping: A ritual act during fire festivals like Beltane, where people would leap over bonfires as a way to cleanse themselves, ensure fertility, and gain protection from evil spirits or bad fortune in the coming year. This act symbolized purification and rebirth.

References

1.   **Hutton, Ronald.** *The Stations of the Sun: A History of the Ritual Year in Britain.* Oxford University Press, 1996.
A comprehensive exploration of the history and transformation of seasonal festivals, including Yule, Samhain, and Beltane, as they evolved from pagan traditions into modern-day holidays.

2.   **Frazer, James George.** *The Golden Bough: A Study in Magic and Religion.* Macmillan, 1922.
This seminal work explores the relationship between myth, ritual, and religion in ancient societies, providing insight into the pagan roots of modern celebrations.

3.   **Baker, Alan R. H.** *Human Sacrifice in Ancient Cultures: Pagan Rites in Myth and History.* Routledge, 2002.
An in-depth look at how human and animal sacrifices were an integral part of ancient religious rites, particularly in harvest and fertility festivals.

4.   **Rogers, Nicholas.** *Halloween: From Pagan Ritual to Party Night.* Oxford University Press, 2002.
A historical examination of Halloween's evolution from the ancient Celtic festival of Samhain into its modern form.

5.   **Miles, Clement A.** *Christmas in Ritual and Tradition, Christian and Pagan.* T. Fisher Unwin, 1912.
A detailed exploration of Christmas traditions and their pagan origins, from Yule to Saturnalia.

6.   **Beard, Mary, et al.** *The Roman Festivals of the Period of the Republic.* Cambridge University Press, 1998.
This work discusses Roman festivals such as Saturnalia, Kalends, and Lupercalia, providing key insights into their chaotic, ritualistic origins and their later transformation.

7. **Paxson, Diana L.** *The Essential Guide to Possession, Depossession, and Divine Relationships.* Red Wheel/Weiser, 2008.
This book offers an in-depth exploration of ancient ritual practices and festivals, focusing on how people engaged with divine and supernatural forces during transitional times of the year.

8. **Pennick, Nigel.** *The Pagan Book of Days: A Guide to the Festivals, Traditions, and Sacred Days of the Year.* Destiny Books, 1992.
A practical guide to the ancient pagan festivals and traditions that have informed modern holidays, from Samhain to Beltane.

9. **Bowman, Marion.** *Belief, Legend, and Custom: The Post-Christian Survival of Ancient Celtic Festivals in Modern Celebrations.* Blackwell, 2004.
Examines how ancient Celtic festivals such as Beltane and Samhain have survived and been repurposed in Christian and modern contexts.

10. **Gordon, Richard L.** *Religion in the Roman Empire: The Material and the Divine.* Blackwell Publishing, 2003.
Discusses Roman religious practices, including Saturnalia and Lupercalia, and their impact on modern holidays such as Christmas and Valentine's Day.

11. **MacDonald, Nathan.** *Not Bread Alone: The Uses of Food in the Old Testament.* Oxford University Press, 2008.
Analyzes the role of harvest festivals and sacrifices in the religious practices of ancient Israel and other early civilizations.

12. **Ellis, Peter Berresford.** *The Druids.* Constable, 1994.
A historical study of Druidic practices and their connection to major Celtic festivals such as Samhain and Beltane, explaining the influence of these traditions on modern holidays.

13.   **Rüpke, Jörg.** *Religion of the Romans.* Polity Press, 2007.
A scholarly look at Roman religious practices and festivals, including the Kalends and Saturnalia, and how they were adapted or erased by Christianity.

14.   **Filoramo, Giovanni.** *A History of Gnosticism.* Blackwell Publishing, 1990.
Discusses the relationship between early Christian beliefs and the pagan festivals they co-opted, shedding light on the transformation of ancient rituals into Christian holidays.

15.   **Green, Miranda J.** *The Gods of the Celts.* Sutton Publishing, 1997.
This book provides a thorough exploration of Celtic deities and the festivals dedicated to them, including Samhain, Beltane, and the harvest rites that influenced modern Halloween and May Day.

16.   **O'Brien, Leslie.** *The Roman Calendar and its Festivals.* Routledge, 2004.
Analyzes the structure of the Roman calendar, including the Kalends and other significant festival days, and their adaptation into Christian holidays.

17.   **Kors, Alan Charles.** *The History of the Occult: Paganism, Magic, and Witchcraft.* Princeton University Press, 1995.
This book covers the historical transformation of pagan magical practices and festivals into the witch-hunts and superstitions that influenced modern holidays like Halloween.

18.   **Henderson, Juliet, and Montserrat Roser-i-Puig.** *Time and Temporalities in European and Chinese Early Empires.* Brill, 2010.
A comparative study on how different ancient cultures, including Rome and China, viewed time and ritual cycles, especially during New Year celebrations.

19.   **Davidson, H. R. Ellis.** *Gods and Myths of Northern Europe.* Penguin Books, 1964.
Explores Norse and Germanic mythology and festivals such

as Yule, connecting these ancient practices to modern Christmas traditions.

20. **Frazer, James George.** *The Worship of Nature.* Macmillan, 1926.

A continuation of Frazer's exploration into the links between nature worship, harvest festivals, and modern holidays, emphasizing the blood rituals and sacrifices that defined early human society.

These references provide a comprehensive foundation for understanding the pagan roots, ritual practices, and later Christian appropriations of the holidays examined in *Blood of the Ancients*. They delve into the ancient myths, blood rituals, and the way religious and social structures have adapted these primal celebrations across time.

Demetri Welsh is not your typical author—he's the voice of the raw, the unapologetic, and the untamed truth. Born into chaos and raised in the shadows of a world that tried to break him, Demetri has spent his life defying every expectation society placed on him. Abandoned by his biological family at the age of two and thrust into a brutal foster care system, Demetri's early years were marked by trauma, abuse, and a constant search for truth in a world that fed him lies.

Despite his dark beginnings, Demetri rose from the ashes, rejecting the religious and societal structures that sought to control him. His rebellious nature and unflinching desire for the truth drove him to delve deep into the realms of the occult, ancient history, and the unseen forces that shape our world. From these studies, he realized that modern life is filled with hidden, forgotten energies that most people are too blind—or too scared—to acknowledge.

As a celebrated psychic reader, energy worker, and musician, Demetri's work transcends the ordinary. He's a man unafraid to confront the controversial, to rip apart the fabric of what we think we know, and reveal the raw, primal forces beneath. His previous books, music, and psychic services have gathered a dedicated following, pulling in seekers from all over the globe—those who crave truth over comfort, and knowledge over ignorance.

Demetri is not just an author, he's a force of nature. With a career that spans from bestselling books to groundbreaking music, everything he touches carries an unmistakable energy—dark, mysterious, provocative, and real. He's here to tell the stories that most are too afraid to face, and *Blood of the Ancients* is no exception. This book is just the latest chapter in his mission to unveil the ancient truths that modern society has buried under centuries of lies, control, and fear.

Demetri currently resides wherever the wind takes him, refusing to be tied down by the chains of convention. He can be found exclusively on Fiverr (@rawveganpsychic), where he offers his psychic readings, alongside his ongoing work as a musician and author. Get ready to be challenged. Get ready to have your reality flipped upside down. Demetri Welsh isn't here to make you comfortable—he's here to wake you the fuck up.